STORYBOARD NOTEBOOK

16:9 Industry Standard | 8.5"x11" Matte Black 4-Panel
Storyboard Sketchbook for Filmmakers & Animators

TABLE OF CONTENTS

SUBJECT/PRODUCTION TITLE	PAGE(S)

STORYBOARD NOTEBOOK

TABLE OF CONTENTS

SUBJECT/PRODUCTION TITLE	PAGE(S)

STORYBOARD NOTEBOOK

SCENE: SHOT: NO.:   SCENE: SHOT: NO.:

SCENE: SHOT: NO.:   SCENE: SHOT: NO.:

PROJECT: DATE:

SCENE: SHOT: NO.:   SCENE: SHOT: NO.:

SCENE: SHOT: NO.:   SCENE: SHOT: NO.:

PROJECT: DATE:

SCENE: SHOT: NO.:   SCENE: SHOT: NO.:

SCENE: SHOT: NO.:   SCENE: SHOT: NO.:

SCENE: SHOT: NO.:   SCENE: SHOT: NO.:

SCENE: SHOT: NO.:   SCENE: SHOT: NO.:

SCENE: SHOT: NO.: SCENE: SHOT: NO.:

SCENE: SHOT: NO.: SCENE: SHOT: NO.:

PROJECT:

DATE:

SCENE: SHOT: NO.: SCENE: SHOT: NO.:

SCENE: SHOT: NO.: SCENE: SHOT: NO.:

STORYBOARD NOTEBOOK

DATE:

SCENE: SHOT: NO.:   SCENE: SHOT: NO.:

SCENE: SHOT: NO.:   SCENE: SHOT: NO.:

PROJECT: [   ] DATE: [   ]

SCENE: SHOT: NO.:   SCENE: SHOT: NO.:

SCENE: SHOT: NO.:   SCENE: SHOT: NO.:

PROJECT: DATE:

SCENE: SHOT: NO.: SCENE: SHOT: NO.:

SCENE: SHOT: NO.: SCENE: SHOT: NO.:

PROJECT: [   ] DATE: [   ]

SCENE: SHOT: NO.:   SCENE: SHOT: NO.:

SCENE: SHOT: NO.:   SCENE: SHOT: NO.:

PROJECT: DATE:

SCENE: SHOT: NO.:   SCENE: SHOT: NO.:

SCENE: SHOT: NO.:   SCENE: SHOT: NO.:

SCENE: SHOT: NO.:   SCENE: SHOT: NO.:

SCENE: SHOT: NO.:   SCENE: SHOT: NO.:

PROJECT: DATE:

SCENE: SHOT: NO.:   SCENE: SHOT: NO.:

SCENE: SHOT: NO.:   SCENE: SHOT: NO.:

PROJECT: DATE:

SCENE: SHOT: NO.: SCENE: SHOT: NO.:

SCENE: SHOT: NO.: SCENE: SHOT: NO.:

SCENE: SHOT: NO.:   SCENE: SHOT: NO.:

SCENE: SHOT: NO.:   SCENE: SHOT: NO.:

SCENE: SHOT: NO.:   SCENE: SHOT: NO.:

SCENE: SHOT: NO.:   SCENE: SHOT: NO.:

PROJECT: [   ]   DATE: [   ]

SCENE: ___   SHOT: ___   NO.: ___   SCENE: ___   SHOT: ___   NO.: ___

SCENE: ___   SHOT: ___   NO.: ___   SCENE: ___   SHOT: ___   NO.: ___

PROJECT: [   ] DATE: [   ]

SCENE: SHOT: NO.:   SCENE: SHOT: NO.:

SCENE: SHOT: NO.:   SCENE: SHOT: NO.:

PROJECT: [   ]   DATE: [   ]

SCENE: SHOT: NO.:   SCENE: SHOT: NO.:

SCENE: SHOT: NO.:   SCENE: SHOT: NO.:

SCENE: SHOT: NO.: SCENE: SHOT: NO.:

SCENE: SHOT: NO.: SCENE: SHOT: NO.:

PROJECT: [_____] DATE: [_____]

SCENE: ___ SHOT: ___ NO.: ___   SCENE: ___ SHOT: ___ NO.: ___

SCENE: ___ SHOT: ___ NO.: ___   SCENE: ___ SHOT: ___ NO.: ___

STORYBOARD NOTEBOOK

SCENE: SHOT: NO.: SCENE: SHOT: NO.:

SCENE: SHOT: NO.: SCENE: SHOT: NO.:

PROJECT: [   ]   DATE: [   ]

SCENE: SHOT: NO.:   SCENE: SHOT: NO.:

SCENE: SHOT: NO.:   SCENE: SHOT: NO.:

PROJECT: |_____| DATE: |_____|

SCENE: SHOT: NO.:   SCENE: SHOT: NO.:

SCENE: SHOT: NO.:   SCENE: SHOT: NO.:

SCENE: SHOT: NO.: SCENE: SHOT: NO.:

SCENE: SHOT: NO.: SCENE: SHOT: NO.:

PROJECT: [   ]   DATE: [   ]

SCENE: _____ SHOT: _____ NO.: _____   SCENE: _____ SHOT: _____ NO.: _____

SCENE: _____ SHOT: _____ NO.: _____   SCENE: _____ SHOT: _____ NO.: _____

DATE:

SCENE: SHOT: NO.: SCENE: SHOT: NO.:

SCENE: SHOT: NO.: SCENE: SHOT: NO.:

PROJECT: DATE:

SCENE: SHOT: NO.: SCENE: SHOT: NO.:

SCENE: SHOT: NO.: SCENE: SHOT: NO.:

PROJECT: [   ]   DATE: [   ]

SCENE: SHOT: NO.:   SCENE: SHOT: NO.:

SCENE: SHOT: NO.:   SCENE: SHOT: NO.:

STORYBOARD NOTEBOOK

PROJECT: [   ]   DATE: [   ]

SCENE: SHOT: NO.:   SCENE: SHOT: NO.:

SCENE: SHOT: NO.:   SCENE: SHOT: NO.:

PROJECT: [   ] DATE: [   ]

SCENE: SHOT: NO.:   SCENE: SHOT: NO.:

SCENE: SHOT: NO.:   SCENE: SHOT: NO.:

PROJECT: [   ]   DATE: [   ]

SCENE: SHOT: NO.:   SCENE: SHOT: NO.:

SCENE: SHOT: NO.:   SCENE: SHOT: NO.:

PROJECT: DATE:

SCENE: SHOT: NO.: SCENE: SHOT: NO.:

SCENE: SHOT: NO.: SCENE: SHOT: NO.:

STORYBOARD NOTEBOOK

PROJECT: [   ] DATE: [   ]

SCENE: SHOT: NO.:   SCENE: SHOT: NO.:

SCENE: SHOT: NO.:   SCENE: SHOT: NO.:

PROJECT: DATE:

SCENE: SHOT: NO.:   SCENE: SHOT: NO.:

SCENE: SHOT: NO.:   SCENE: SHOT: NO.:

STORYBOARD NOTEBOOK

PROJECT: DATE:

SCENE: SHOT: NO.:   SCENE: SHOT: NO.:

SCENE: SHOT: NO.:   SCENE: SHOT: NO.:

SCENE:　　　SHOT:　　　NO.:　　　SCENE:　　　SHOT:　　　NO.:

SCENE:　　　SHOT:　　　NO.:　　　SCENE:　　　SHOT:　　　NO.:

PROJECT: [   ]   DATE: [   ]

SCENE: SHOT: NO.:   SCENE: SHOT: NO.:

SCENE: SHOT: NO.:   SCENE: SHOT: NO.:

PROJECT: _____ DATE: _____

SCENE: _____ SHOT: _____ NO.: _____   SCENE: _____ SHOT: _____ NO.: _____

SCENE: _____ SHOT: _____ NO.: _____   SCENE: _____ SHOT: _____ NO.: _____

STORYBOARD NOTEBOOK

PROJECT: DATE:

SCENE: SHOT: NO.: SCENE: SHOT: NO.:

SCENE: SHOT: NO.: SCENE: SHOT: NO.:

PROJECT: DATE:

SCENE: SHOT: NO.:

SCENE: SHOT: NO.:

SCENE: SHOT: NO.:

SCENE: SHOT: NO.:

PROJECT: [   ] DATE: [   ]

SCENE: SHOT: NO.:   SCENE: SHOT: NO.:

SCENE: SHOT: NO.:   SCENE: SHOT: NO.:

PROJECT: [   ] DATE: [   ]

SCENE: SHOT: NO.:   SCENE: SHOT: NO.:

SCENE: SHOT: NO.:   SCENE: SHOT: NO.:

PROJECT: [   ] DATE: [   ]

SCENE: SHOT: NO.:   SCENE: SHOT: NO.:

SCENE: SHOT: NO.:   SCENE: SHOT: NO.:

DATE:

SCENE: SHOT: NO.:   SCENE: SHOT: NO.:

SCENE: SHOT: NO.:   SCENE: SHOT: NO.:

PROJECT: DATE:

SCENE: SHOT: NO.: SCENE: SHOT: NO.:

SCENE: SHOT: NO.: SCENE: SHOT: NO.:

PROJECT: **DATE:**

SCENE: SHOT: NO.:   SCENE: SHOT: NO.:

SCENE: SHOT: NO.:   SCENE: SHOT: NO.:

PROJECT: [   ] DATE: [   ]

SCENE: SHOT: NO.:   SCENE: SHOT: NO.:

SCENE: SHOT: NO.:   SCENE: SHOT: NO.:

SCENE: SHOT: NO.: SCENE: SHOT: NO.:

SCENE: SHOT: NO.: SCENE: SHOT: NO.:

PROJECT: [   ]   DATE: [   ]

SCENE: _____ SHOT: _____ NO.: _____   SCENE: _____ SHOT: _____ NO.: _____

SCENE: _____ SHOT: _____ NO.: _____   SCENE: _____ SHOT: _____ NO.: _____

STORYBOARD NOTEBOOK   **57**

PROJECT: [   ] DATE: [   ]

SCENE: SHOT: NO.:   SCENE: SHOT: NO.:

SCENE: SHOT: NO.:   SCENE: SHOT: NO.:

PROJECT: _____ DATE: _____

SCENE: _____ SHOT: _____ NO.: _____   SCENE: _____ SHOT: _____ NO.: _____

SCENE: _____ SHOT: _____ NO.: _____   SCENE: _____ SHOT: _____ NO.: _____

PROJECT: DATE:

SCENE: SHOT: NO.: SCENE: SHOT: NO.:

SCENE: SHOT: NO.: SCENE: SHOT: NO.:

STORYBOARD NOTEBOOK

PROJECT: [   ]   DATE: [   ]

SCENE: SHOT: NO.:   SCENE: SHOT: NO.:

SCENE: SHOT: NO.:   SCENE: SHOT: NO.:

PROJECT: [   ]   DATE: [   ]

SCENE: SHOT: NO.:   SCENE: SHOT: NO.:

SCENE: SHOT: NO.:   SCENE: SHOT: NO.:

PROJECT: [   ]   DATE: [   ]

SCENE: SHOT: NO.:   SCENE: SHOT: NO.:

SCENE: SHOT: NO.:   SCENE: SHOT: NO.:

SCENE: SHOT: NO.: SCENE: SHOT: NO.:

SCENE: SHOT: NO.: SCENE: SHOT: NO.:

SCENE: SHOT: NO.: SCENE: SHOT: NO.:

SCENE: SHOT: NO.: SCENE: SHOT: NO.:

PROJECT: DATE:

SCENE: SHOT: NO.: SCENE: SHOT: NO.:

SCENE: SHOT: NO.: SCENE: SHOT: NO.:

SCENE: SHOT: NO.: SCENE: SHOT: NO.:

SCENE: SHOT: NO.: SCENE: SHOT: NO.:

SCENE: SHOT: NO.:   SCENE: SHOT: NO.:

SCENE: SHOT: NO.:   SCENE: SHOT: NO.:

PROJECT: DATE:

SCENE: SHOT: NO.: SCENE: SHOT: NO.:

SCENE: SHOT: NO.: SCENE: SHOT: NO.:

PROJECT: DATE:

SCENE: SHOT: NO.:   SCENE: SHOT: NO.:

SCENE: SHOT: NO.:   SCENE: SHOT: NO.:

STORYBOARD NOTEBOOK

PROJECT: [   ]   DATE: [   ]

SCENE: SHOT: NO.:   SCENE: SHOT: NO.:

SCENE: SHOT: NO.:   SCENE: SHOT: NO.:

SCENE: SHOT: NO.:   SCENE: SHOT: NO.:

SCENE: SHOT: NO.:   SCENE: SHOT: NO.:

PROJECT: [   ]   DATE: [   ]

SCENE: _____ SHOT: _____ NO.: _____   SCENE: _____ SHOT: _____ NO.: _____

SCENE: _____ SHOT: _____ NO.: _____   SCENE: _____ SHOT: _____ NO.: _____

SCENE: SHOT: NO.:   SCENE: SHOT: NO.:

SCENE: SHOT: NO.:   SCENE: SHOT: NO.:

PROJECT: [   ]   DATE: [   ]

SCENE: SHOT: NO.:   SCENE: SHOT: NO.:

SCENE: SHOT: NO.:   SCENE: SHOT: NO.:

SCENE: SHOT: NO.: SCENE: SHOT: NO.:

SCENE: SHOT: NO.: SCENE: SHOT: NO.:

SCENE: SHOT: NO.: SCENE: SHOT: NO.:

SCENE: SHOT: NO.: SCENE: SHOT: NO.:

PROJECT: _____ DATE: _____

SCENE: _____ SHOT: _____ NO.: _____   SCENE: _____ SHOT: _____ NO.: _____

SCENE: _____ SHOT: _____ NO.: _____   SCENE: _____ SHOT: _____ NO.: _____

STORYBOARD NOTEBOOK

DATE:

SCENE: SHOT: NO.:   SCENE: SHOT: NO.:

SCENE: SHOT: NO.:   SCENE: SHOT: NO.:

PROJECT: [   ]   DATE: [   ]

SCENE: _____   SHOT: _____   NO.: _____   SCENE: _____   SHOT: _____   NO.: _____

SCENE: _____   SHOT: _____   NO.: _____   SCENE: _____   SHOT: _____   NO.: _____

STORYBOARD NOTEBOOK

SCENE: SHOT: NO.:   SCENE: SHOT: NO.:

SCENE: SHOT: NO.:   SCENE: SHOT: NO.:

PROJECT:

DATE:

SCENE: SHOT: NO.:   SCENE: SHOT: NO.:

SCENE: SHOT: NO.:   SCENE: SHOT: NO.:

PROJECT: [   ] DATE: [   ]

SCENE: SHOT: NO.:   SCENE: SHOT: NO.:

SCENE: SHOT: NO.:   SCENE: SHOT: NO.:

PROJECT: **DATE:**

SCENE: SHOT: NO.:   SCENE: SHOT: NO.:

SCENE: SHOT: NO.:   SCENE: SHOT: NO.:

PROJECT: [   ]   DATE: [   ]

SCENE: SHOT: NO.:   SCENE: SHOT: NO.:

SCENE: SHOT: NO.:   SCENE: SHOT: NO.:

SCENE: SHOT: NO.: SCENE: SHOT: NO.:

SCENE: SHOT: NO.: SCENE: SHOT: NO.:

PROJECT: 　　　　　　　　　　　　　DATE:

SCENE: 　　　SHOT: 　　　NO.: 　　　SCENE: 　　　SHOT: 　　　NO.:

SCENE: 　　　SHOT: 　　　NO.: 　　　SCENE: 　　　SHOT: 　　　NO.:

PROJECT: DATE:

SCENE: SHOT: NO.:   SCENE: SHOT: NO.:

SCENE: SHOT: NO.:   SCENE: SHOT: NO.:

PROJECT: [_____]   DATE: [_____]

SCENE: _____   SHOT: _____   NO.: _____   SCENE: _____   SHOT: _____   NO.: _____

SCENE: _____   SHOT: _____   NO.: _____   SCENE: _____   SHOT: _____   NO.: _____

PROJECT: DATE:

SCENE: SHOT: NO.: SCENE: SHOT: NO.:

SCENE: SHOT: NO.: SCENE: SHOT: NO.:

PROJECT:

DATE:

SCENE: SHOT: NO.: SCENE: SHOT: NO.:

SCENE: SHOT: NO.: SCENE: SHOT: NO.:

PROJECT: [   ] DATE: [   ]

SCENE: SHOT: NO.:   SCENE: SHOT: NO.:

SCENE: SHOT: NO.:   SCENE: SHOT: NO.:

PROJECT: [   ]   DATE: [   ]

SCENE: SHOT: NO.:   SCENE: SHOT: NO.:

SCENE: SHOT: NO.:   SCENE: SHOT: NO.:

PROJECT: [   ]   DATE: [   ]

SCENE: SHOT: NO.:   SCENE: SHOT: NO.:

SCENE: SHOT: NO.:   SCENE: SHOT: NO.:

STORYBOARD NOTEBOOK

PROJECT: _____   DATE: _____

SCENE: _____ SHOT: _____ NO.: _____   SCENE: _____ SHOT: _____ NO.: _____

SCENE: _____ SHOT: _____ NO.: _____   SCENE: _____ SHOT: _____ NO.: _____

Made in the USA
Las Vegas, NV
24 May 2021